DANCE ANGLES

A DANCE PACK FOR 7 – 11 YEAR OLDS

Rosie Thorner   Music by Dominic Sandford

SOUTHGATE

First published 2006 by Southgate Publishers Ltd
Reprinted 2009

Southgate Publishers Ltd
The Square, Sandford, Crediton, Devon EX17 4LW

Printed and bound in Great Britain by ImprintDigital, Upton Pyne, Devon, UK

British Library Cataloguing in Publication Data.
A CIP catalogue record for this book is available from the British Library.

ISBN 1–85741–101–3
ISBN 9781857411010

Acknowledgements

Page 33; extract from Chapter 6, The Sea-Hag, taken from the book Beowolf by Rosemary Sutcliff, published by Red Fox.
Mrs Jacky King and the children at Charlton Mackrell School.
Mrs Terrie Elliss

How to deliver quality dance lessons

Our courses help teachers to build up dance resources and their own confidence in order to deliver dance lessons that will:
- help each child to further their potential
- work at a pace suitable to both teacher and child
- maximize the learning experience of each theme.

Courses offer step-by-step guidance on how to deliver and develop dance at Key Stages 1 and 2 and for Early Years.

The courses include the following areas:
- warm-ups
- introducing a theme to complement curriculum study and making it move!
- development and progression of themes
- differentiation, evaluation and performance.

For more information please contact:

✳ www.danceangles.com
✳ Tel: 01458 224573
✳ info@danceangles.com

Dance Angles

CONTENTS

Introduction:

Warm-ups:

The Dance Themes:

Glossary:

A list of terms to aid an understanding of dance.

Appendix:

Cue cards

A music CD (warm-ups plus 8 unique soundtracks to accompany the programme of study and lesson plans).

INTRODUCTION

Why Dance?

Dance has many physical benefits: it encourages good posture; body tension; body awareness; rhythm; co-ordination; balance; control and timing.

It also has a positive effect on confidence, spatial awareness and creativity.

In a class situation it allows children to burn off excess energy in a constructive manner, while the mind runs riot in a controlled way!

Dance is accessible to everyone, and can be a positive experience for all children, regardless of gender or ability.

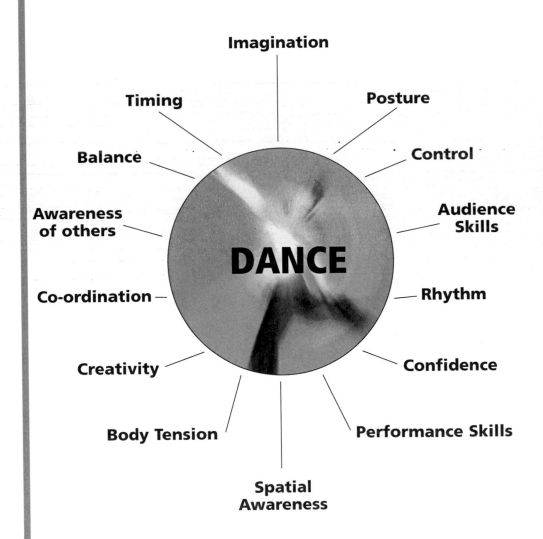

DANCE ANGLES

What will be achieved?

DANCE IN THE CURRICULUM

Dance has an important place in the delivery of two hours of quality P.E. a week. It captures the attention of all children, enabling them to achieve success. Dance is inclusive; it provides an opportunity for less able children to shine, particularly those who cannot express themselves through writing or speech.

It is also an excellent cross-curricular tool. Use it to link subjects with a topic or to corroborate learning with a fresh perspective. Develop a poem with dance, e.g. fire, and reinforce it in art with costume and make-up. It can be used to support work in maths, e.g. time; to enhance general topics, e.g. the sea; to complement study of a book, e.g. Beowulf "Dragonslayer"; or simply to mark festivals, e.g. bonfire night.

Both indoor and outdoor space can be used for dance, regardless of its size. Dance requires no equipment or mats, just space. All hazards should be identified and obstructions removed.

Attainment Levels for Key Stage 2 in P.E.

Knowledge, skills and understanding:

Teaching should ensure that when evaluating and improving performance, connections are made between developing, selecting and applying skills, tactics and compositional ideas, and fitness and health.

The Key Stage 2 programme of study for Physical Education lists attainment levels and targets. These targets are cross-referenced throughout the book to highlight the learning outcome for each lesson. The programme of study states that pupils should be taught:

1. Acquiring and developing skills
   a) consolidate their existing skills and gain new ones
   b) perform actions and skills with more consistent control and quality.

2. Selecting and applying skills, tactics and compositional ideas
   a) plan, use and adapt strategies, tactics and compositional ideas for individual, pair, small-group and small-team activities
   b) develop and use their knowledge of the principles behind the strategies, tactics and ideas to improve their effectiveness
   c) apply rules and conventions for different activities.

3. Evaluating and improving performance
   a) identify what makes a performance effective
   b) suggest improvements based on this information.

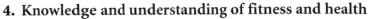

4. **Knowledge and understanding of fitness and health**
   a) how exercise affects the body in the short term
   b) to warm up and prepare appropriately for different activities
   c) why physical activity is good for their health and well-being
   d) why wearing appropriate clothing and being hygienic is good for
      their health and safety.

5. **Breadth of study**
   No direct reference is made to this area of study.

6. **Dance activities**
   a) create and perform dances using a range of movement patterns,
      including those from different times, places and cultures
   b) respond to a range of stimuli and accompaniment.

These attainment levels are cross referenced throughout this book, to high-light the learning outcome for each phase.

End of Key Stage 2 Targets

Level 3
- Pupils should be able to select and use actions and ideas appropriately, applying them with co-ordination and control.
- They should understand composition by starting to vary how they respond.
- They can see how their work is similar to and different from others' work, and use this to improve their own performance.
- They should understand the reasons for warm-up, and why physical activity is good for health.

Level 4
- Pupils link skills, actions and apply them accurately and appropriately.
- Their performance shows precision, control and fluency, and they understand composition.
- They are able to compare and comment on ideas used in their own and others' work, and use this understanding to improve performance.
- They are able to explain and apply basic safe warm-up. They can describe the effect of exercise on the body, and on health.

Level 5
- Pupils select and combine ideas and apply them appropriately, consistently showing precision, control and fluency.
- They should draw on their knowledge about composition when performing.
- They should analyse and comment on techniques and how these are applied to their own and others' work. They should modify and refine to improve performance.
- They can explain the body's reaction to exercise and why it is good for health. They select relevant warm-up and cool-down methods.

Dance at home

Pupils should be encouraged to share what they have learned at home. They may wish to perform dances, and to teach them to family and friends, so that everyone can join in this fun way to keep fit! Similarly, they may be inspired to join a local dance or dance/drama class to further their participation in dance.

How to use the pack

The pack has been designed by a teacher, for teachers. It will enable non-specialist teachers to explore dance through a wide variety of themes and topics, and gives guidance on how to initiate, teach and develop lessons at KS2. The music CD, lesson plans and cue cards are designed to maximize the learning experience for the pupils, and provide the teacher with all the material needed to teach dance successfully. The themes have been tried and tested in many primary schools, with very positive results.

THE THEMES

Each of the eight themes explores topics which are common to everyday life, the world around us, historical events or fictional stories, and includes some traditional dance ideas. The wide selection of topics gives an illustration of the flexibility of dance in the curriculum. There are examples of different dance styles within this resource, ranging from structured phrases to abstract improvisation and dance drama. Each theme can be delivered as a separate entity, or as a scheme of work.

The themes are each divided into three or four phases, designed to enable pupils gradually to develop a movement vocabulary and work towards a performance. The content of each theme is divided into phases as opposed to lessons, to encourage teachers to develop their own style and pace without restriction.

It is possible, however, to choose one theme and explore it in a workshop. Either condense the work, or focus on a specific area, for an intense experience culminating in a performance. This can be dramatic and exciting, with very visible progress and a greater emphasis on performance skills.

All themes could be used, in any order, throughout the entire Key Stage.

Each of the detailed phases relates directly to KS2 attainment levels, denoted by the criterion reference, e.g. 6a. This highlights the learning outcomes experienced in each lesson.

When you have decided upon which theme to explore, try to read through the material, keeping in mind the space that you are going to use and the group of children you are teaching. Make yourself familiar with the outline

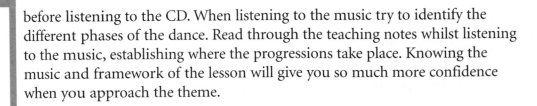

before listening to the CD. When listening to the music try to identify the different phases of the dance. Read through the teaching notes whilst listening to the music, establishing where the progressions take place. Knowing the music and framework of the lesson will give you so much more confidence when you approach the theme.

THE MUSIC

The music has been written specifically for dance teachers. It is unique and designed to provoke creativity. The short pieces of music have no lyrics (to limit preconceived ideas of pop dance routines). Each piece has a very definite beat and tempo. The pieces demonstrate clear changes, e.g. quiet to loud and hard to soft, which are easily recognizable.

The tracks can be used as a whole, for working towards a performance, or in sections to develop step patterns or individual ideas. The music can be used to inspire other dance/movement ideas, or simply to add atmosphere to topic discussions.

CUE CARDS

An additional teaching aid is the cue cards. These are used as a stimulus or framework on which to build and develop a movement vocabulary. They can be used for individual or group work. The cue cards are located in the Appendix, and are presented in the form of a list of words and pictures. Select the cues which are relevant to the dance you are working on. Photocopy, enlarge and cut out the words, or write them in large, clear writing on a piece of card. It is a good idea to laminate the cards so that they can be frequently used. Cue cards can be interchanged with each dance, and you may feel like adding some of your own.

Using the resource pack will give you confidence to explore dance further and increase the pupils' experience of dance. It can also be used as a platform to develop other themes within the same framework. Above all, have fun and enjoy the movement!

WARM-UPS

Why warm up?

This is an essential part of any physical lesson, and a good practice to adopt. It allows an increased blood flow to the muscles, which helps to avoid injury and improve suppleness and flexibility.

A warm-up can be used to introduce related ideas to the topic or to work on specific group needs, e.g. spatial awareness. It can also be used to remind pupils of previous work covered, thus reinforcing their movement vocabulary.

Warm-up activities can be used to expend excess energy, to allow concentration on the lesson content. Improvements in rhythm and timing will help in other areas of life, e.g. posture, co-ordination and confidence. Improvements have been noticed in other sporting areas as well as in the classroom.

A dance warm-up is the ideal time to focus on the reasons why exercise is good for us. Similarly, an understanding of why we have bare feet and wear loose clothing to dance can be demonstrated and reinforced on a regular basis.

4a How exercise affects the body in the short term

4b To warm up and prepare appropriately for different activities

4c Why physical activity is good for their health and well-being.
4d Why wearing appropriate clothing and being hygienic is good for their health and safety

What is a warm-up?

- Children should ideally have bare feet to avoid slipping and ensure maximum movement and flexibility.

- They should begin in space, not touching each other, walls or equipment or near any hazards.

- The aim is to build a warm-up movement vocabulary, which can include ideas for creative work, revisit previous work or focus on areas of interest, e.g. flexibility or strength.

- Initially use gentle static movements to 'wake up the body and mind'.

- Movements should start small and soft, progressing to large and heavy.

- Aim to increase size, intensity and speed of movement.

- Take each movement as far as is comfortable. There should never be any discomfort or pain. Encourage children to hold the stretch position for three seconds. Explain that flexibility will increase when exercises are repeated.

4a How exercise affects the body in the short term.

Use of music

Ideally, a relaxing accompaniment with no lyrics enables complete focus on movement. Similarly, a flowing piece will encourage gentle beginnings and concentrate thought. Use a track which is familiar or one which is being used currently by the class in another curriculum area. Alternatively, use the dance CD to revise previous phases of study.

Suggested exercises

- Movements should start from the top of the body and work down.

- Focus on waking up each individual part of the body in isolation, e.g. head; neck; trunk; back; abdomen; hips; legs; knees and ankles.

- For each joint or muscle area start slowly and build up, e.g. gentle flex and point of the ankle joint leading to bouncing and low, light jumps.

- It is important to concentrate on correct posture and to develop an understanding of centring (centre of balance) and rotation.

- Safe exercise and the correct use of muscles and joints should be emphasised.

- Focus on control: this can be in terms of body tension, spatial awareness and enthusiasm.

- The cardiovascular aspect of the warm-up can be covered by light, easy travelling. This can incorporate restricted changes in direction, level and speed and include jumps and spins. It is essential to consider the class management of travel, so that all work is constructive and safe.

- Developing a warm-up routine or pattern, which is used prior to each dance lesson, will enable the children to develop confidence and build up a movement vocabulary.

- In addition to a general, regular warm-up, it is beneficial to include movements or exercises relevant to the lesson that will follow.

- The length of warm-up will depend on a variety of factors, e.g. the temperature of the room, the time of day, the previous activity, and the intensity of the lesson content to follow. However, the warm-up should always last at least five minutes.

THE DANCE THEMES

Fire

(Inspired by The Great Fire of London)

WARM-UP

- Move in a space – slow, soft footsteps, changing direction.
- Introduce travel in curved lines as the flames explore everything in their path. Footsteps get heavier and faster, stride length longer and stronger.
- Focus on individual body parts, starting with slow, soft movements and building to strong large ones.

FIRE

Slowly starting with a **flicker**,
Fiercely starts to grow,
Hissing and **spitting**, the flames take hold,
Dancing, twisting up and down.

Leaping, writhing, devouring all in its path,
Darting and **turning** high and low,
Then the **energy** runs out,
There's nothing left to burn.

A **crackle** and **hiss**, the fire goes out,
Behind it the trail of burnt charcoal,
And the cruel smell of loss.

6a Responding to stimuli by making imaginative shapes.

Talk about the words used to describe fire in the poem. There are cue cards available (page 62). Are there any other words you can think of?

Initial sparks flicker then die, flicker then die, until they have enough energy and are large enough to ignite the fire. Explore the idea of the initial spark. Make a quick, sharp, flicking movement, which disappears almost immediately. A similar movement, from either the same body part or a different one, follows this.

Use 'body part' cue cards (page 68) to help pupils focus on isolated movements: toes, foot, ankle, knee, hip, fingers, hand, wrist, elbow, shoulder and head. Allow the pupils to work as individuals to experiment with three body parts of their choice. Aim for the movements to be short and soft, but clearly visible.

1a - consolidate existing skills and gain new ones.

PROGRESSION

In pairs, pupils should show each other their individual movements. Suggest that each pupil mirrors their partner's movements (reciprocal teaching). Encourage pairs to use contrasting movements, e.g. up/down, left/right, inwards/outwards. Allow time for them to practise and develop a phrase involving a combination of mirroring and contrasting movements.

1b/2a Perform actions with more control and quality./Plan compositional ideas in pairs.

6a Create and perform a range of movement patterns.

2b Develop and use knowledge of the principles behind the ideas to improve their effectiveness.

DIFFERENTIATION

Some children may wish to concentrate more fully on the timing and quality of a small number of movements. Others may relish the challenge of developing more detailed movement patterns with a partner.

DEVELOPMENT

Explore the concept of the growing fire as it increases in energy and spreads. Pairs can experiment with larger, stronger movements, which are longer-lasting. They can use the same body parts, or try some new ones. They could link two parts in one movement, e.g. an arm thrusting upward (flame), while the fingers move (sparks).

Encourage exploration of changes in level and width. Pupils' shapes should grow taller and wider to express the increasing ferocity of the fire. If pupils began on the floor they should be moving towards crouching and then standing at this point.

Fire

WARM-UP

The Fire Game: Divide the room into four areas: sparks, flames, inferno, embers. Ask the pupils to move as if they were water (a) in a bucket; (b) a trickle from a hose; or (c) full power from a hose. Give instructions: e.g. inferno and bucket; sparks and trickle… Watch how they move.

INFERNO

Recap the flame and **flame/travel sequences** – initially, without music. Encourage children to work at their own pace, focusing on movement quality.

Explain that the fire started with individuals making small, quick movements and progressed through pairs and then groups making larger, more dramatic movements. As a class, think of ways to work together to illustrate the fire at its maximum power – the inferno stage.

1b Perform actions with more consistent quality and control.

Take lots of children's ideas and encourage everyone to experiment with them. Let the class decide which movements are most effective and practise them as a group.

3a/b Identify what makes a good performance./Suggest improvements based on this.

PROGRESSION

Experiment with the group shape and point of focus, e.g. does the class wish to be in a circle facing inwards or lines facing the front? Discuss group dynamics, such as the front people performing at low level, those in the middle at medium level and those at the back at high level.

2c Apply styles for different activities/positions.

DIFFERENTIATION

When the **inferno sequence** has been decided, some pupils may want to make modifications, e.g. performing it while seated, inverting it, widening it, or performing it as a canon. Others may wish to perform the basics very effectively.

DEVELOPMENT

Put the Fire Dance together from start to finish with accompaniment. Decide how to end the dance sequence. Suggest that as the fire runs out of energy the shapes and movements should reflect this, possibly ending as still, lifeless embers on the floor. A chaotic, unstructured final class shape would demonstrate the devastating effect of fire. A mass of uneven, ragged, jagged bodies would illustrate the destructive nature of fire and the cruel smell of loss.

6a/b Create and perform dances using a range of movement patterns./Respond to a range of stimuli and accompaniment.

Notation

Sparks	individual	low level, small, quick movements
Igniting	pairs	growing in height/ width mirror/contrast
Flame sequence	small groups	canon – spreading
Flame travel sequence	small groups	follow leader/ move in space
Inferno	whole class	peak of fire – strong, big, fast movements
Embers	whole class	out of energy – fades

Musical structure

Sparks
00 – 30sec.
Sparking and dying … sparking and dying … flickering.

Igniting
31 – 48sec.
Igniting into flames, flicking and spreading.

Movement time
49 – 58sec.

Flame sequence
59sec. – 1min. 46sec.

Flame travel sequence
1min. 47sec. – 2min. 04sec.
Growing more ferocious as the fire takes hold: dancing; twisting; leaping; writhing; devouring.

Inferno
2min. 05sec. – 3min. 29sec.
The fire at its most powerful and devastating.

Embers
3min. 30sec. – 4min. 18sec.
Running out of energy – nothing left to burn. With a crackle and a hiss, the fire goes out. Eerie, soft music towards a fade-out.

This is quite a rigid structure. With some groups it may be more appropriate to allow them to determine the phases and changes within the music themselves. Suggest that pupils use cues such as an increase in tempo, or the sounds of bells or drumbeats to identify each section. Freedom to interpret the music and to respond independently to it will have a positive effect on the quality of performance. However, some pupils will require a clear framework in which to feel safe and confident enough to achieve.

6b Respond to a range of stimuli and accompaniment.

The Pied Piper

(Inspired by *The Pied Piper of Hamelin* by Robert Browning)

Into the street the Piper stept,
    Smiling first a little smile,
As if he knew what magic slept
    In his quiet pipe the while;
Then, like a musical adept,
To blow the pipe his lips he wrinkled,
And green and blue his sharp eyes twinkled,
Like a candle flame where salt is sprinkled;
And ere three shrill notes the pipe uttered,
You heard as if an army muttered;
And muttering grew to a grumbling;
And the grumbling grew to a mighty rumbling;
And out of the houses the rats came tumbling.
Great rats, small rats, lean rats, brawny rats,
Brown rats, black rats, grey rats, tawny rats,
Grave old plodders, gay young friskers,
Fathers, mothers, uncles, cousins,
Cocking tails and pricking whiskers,
    Families by tens and dozens,
Brothers, sisters, husbands, wives –
Followed the Piper for their lives.
From street to street he piped advancing,
And step by step they followed dancing,
Until they came to the river Weser,
    Wherein all plunged and perished!

Warm-up

Street games that children used to play:
- **Skipping** – on the spot; moving in different directions; two feet; one foot; high knees; fast and slow.
- **Football** – raise knees to play 'keepie up'; lunge to reach a ball; swing legs forwards and backwards to kick for goal; head the ball.
- **Cricket** – throw the ball by circling arms slowly forward and then jog to get the ball; stretch to catch to one side; catch to the other.

Rats

Discuss what it would have been like to live in Brunswick town in 1376. How would the children's lives be different from today? What do the children know about rats? Why were they there and in such great numbers?

Consider the features of rats: small pointed faces; beady eyes; sharp teeth; hairy bodies; long tails; small, fast-moving feet. Explore the mannerisms of a rat: cleaning its face with its feet; scratching itself and the things around it; biting; twitching its nose; flicking its long tail and rolling to get its food.

1a Consolidate existing skills and gain new ones.

Ask the pupils to scratch, wash and eat like a rat. Remember that in dance, movements need to be exaggerated (larger and slower) to emphasize the activity.

PROGRESSION

1b/2a Perform actions with more control and quality./Plan compositional ideas in pairs.

Develop a selection of motifs that express the habits of a rat. Use lots of the pupils' ideas and try out, modify and practise them as isolated motifs. Pair the pupils up; ask them to teach each other and improve each other's skills (reciprocal teaching).

DIFFERENTIATION

Notation for a **Rat phrase** is included on page 22. If a group is lacking ideas at the initial stage it may be useful to demonstrate this. Some children may wish to extract from this, while others will enjoy the challenge of finding new motifs.

3a/b Identify what makes a performance effective. Suggest improvements based on this information.

Demonstrate the children's favourites and discuss what makes them good. How can the motif be modified so that everyone can perform it successfully?

DEVELOPMENT

Choose four motifs to link together in a class **Rat phrase**. The children may decide the order and how they link together. Note that the start and finish positions must be the same so that the phrase can be repeated.

Divide the class into four groups and allow each group time to work as a team, perfecting the movement quality and timing of the phrase. Use a count of 8 and encourage the children to count as they move.

Arrange the groups at separate sides of the room. Label the groups 1-4. Each group has a count of 8 to move into the centre of the room, the children then perform their motif (count of 8) and leave the centre (count of 8). As Group 1 are leaving, Group 2 are entering, and so on until all groups have performed. Entering and leaving should be like rats scampering. This style of movement is known as a canon, as it is repeated one after another.

6a Create and perform a range of movement patterns.

This phrase illustrates the movement of thousands and thousands of rats which kept emerging from buildings to follow the piper.

The Pied Piper

WARM-UP
- Static stretches involving the whole body.
- Revise the **Rat phrase**. Mark it through initially to remind the children, then walk, and increase until at full pace.

MOVING LIKE RATS
Listen to the CD and identify the section where the rats are scampering and moving haphazardly about.

6b Respond to accompaniment.

Explore the movement of rats. Get the pupils to try scampering lightly on tiptoe; making quick darting movements, changing direction at speed; leaping from one foot to two; spinning and rolling to escape capture.

This is the less structured, expressive part of the dance. Ask the pupils to experiment with moving on light tiptoe whilst in a curled shape, close to the ground; then a medium-level shape; a wide shape; a tall, wide shape; and a tall, thin shape. This communicates the idea of rats of different shapes and sizes.

PROGRESSION
Consider take-offs and landings as the rats leap over everything in their path… including each other! Variations can include taking off on one leg and landing on two; keeping knees high; separating legs or doing a twist in the middle. Experiment with one foot to one foot; two feet to two feet; and two feet to one foot.

If there are any stage blocks or stable benches (safety is vital here, of course), find interesting ways of getting on to them and using the extra height when jumping off. Similarly, pupils could leapfrog over each other.

Get them to experiment with controlled spins and rolls, being aware of hard floors and others around them.

TEACHING POINT
Teach the pupils always to bend knees on landing for safety, silence and good presentation. When leapfrogging, the person being leapt over should have chin down towards chest, firm flat back supported by two hands on thighs, knees bent, legs shoulder width apart.

2b Develop and use knowledge of principles behind ideas to improve effectiveness.

DIFFERENTIATION
Control and spatial awareness are very important in this type of 'free' activity. It is essential to demand safe practice, but at the same time encourage individuality and creativity. Some children may feel self-conscious in such unstructured situations and others may lack ideas and simply prefer to follow instructions.

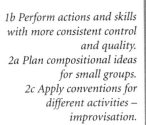

1b Perform actions and skills with more consistent control and quality.
2a Plan compositional ideas for small groups.
2c Apply conventions for different activities – improvisation.

3a/b Identify what makes a performance effective./Suggest improvements based on this.

DEVELOPMENT

Using the **Scampering phases** within the music, encourage the pupils to move on to a designated stage area from any point around the room, using as much space as possible and any raised areas. Encourage them to link different types of movements, e.g. a jump from one foot to two, followed by a spin and then a leap with straddled legs. Two children may wish to meet at a designated point to perform a leapfrog.

Divide the class into the same four groups as before. Ask the pupils to observe performances and to advise each other on how to improve presentation, e.g. changes in level, moving at a variety of low, medium and high levels. Similarly, they should consider use of space; it may be noticed that a large number of pupils congregate in one area, leaving another empty.

The Pied Piper

WARM-UP

- Beginning with the head, pupils should wake up each body part individually. Start with small, slow, light movements, gradually increasing size, speed and strength.
- Move on toes around the room, using light, quick darting movements, changing direction quickly into space. Spin and jump with care and control.
- Recap the **Rat and Scampering phrase** – initially without music. Encourage pupils to work at their own pace, focusing on movement quality. With the music, allow the children to identify and move in the correct phases.

1b Perform actions with more consistent quality and control.

INTRODUCE THE PIPER

Using a flute, recorder or cardboard cut-out of a pipe, illustrate how the piper may have moved. Ask the pupils to join in skipping, spinning and pretending to play a pipe.

Piper motif: skip forward to the right (two steps); skip forward to the left (two steps); spin 360 degrees anticlockwise (four steps). Point the pipe to the direction of movement on the skips.

1a Consolidate existing skills and gain new ones.

PROGRESSION

Pupils work in the same four groups as in the **Rat phrase**. Choose one in each group to be the piper, while the rest of the group move around him/her, performing their **Scampering phrase**. Rotate the piper so that everyone has a turn.

6a Create and perform dances using a range of movement patterns.

THE PIED PIPER DANCE

Put the Pied Piper Dance together from start to finish, with accompaniment.

6a/b Create and perform dances using a range of movement patterns./Respond to a range of intensity within accompaniment and increasing group size.

DIFFERENTIATION

It is possible to perform this as a class dance, with one individual selected as the piper. However, some children may be lost in the large number involved and may prefer to perform in small groups, each group having a piper.

2c Apply rules for different activities.

DEVELOPMENT

The Piper enters first, followed by the **Rat phrase**. Decide from which side the Piper should enter and exit, or whether he/she should stay to pipe during the phrase. This is followed by the **Scampering phrase**, which includes the Piper performing the **Piper Motif**.

The finale of the dance is slower and more sombre, illustrating the final passage of the rats to their death. Decide how to end the dance sequence. Suggest that as all the rats come to a watery end in the River Weser, pupils may wish to take movements from either the **Rat** or the **Scampering phrase** and alter them for this section. Movements could be slowed or moved forwards (possibly in one direction as if towards the river, following the Piper).

2b Develop and use knowledge of the principles behind ideas to improve their effectiveness.

Alternatively, a completely new motif could be developed and perfected. It may be best for all to exit the stage at the same side, leaving only the piper to wind his merry way back to the village and out of sight.

Costume: pupils could make their own rat masks and long tails to help them get into character.

Musical structure

0 – 20sec.	**Introduction (Piper motif)**
21 – 56sec.	**Rat phrase – canon**
	Gp 1 on motif x 2 – off
	Gp 2
	Gp 3
	Gp 4
	Gps 1 + 2 on motif x 2 – off
	Gps 3 + 4

	Gp 1 on motif	**x 5**
	Gp 2	**x 4**
	Gp 3	**x 3**
	Gp 4	**x 2**

57sec. – 1min. 47sec.	**Scampering phrase + Piper motif**
1min. 48sec. – 2min. 44sec.	**Finale**

Notation

Rat phrase
Wipe face (back of hand) L + R
2 hands in front of chest – 4 quick steps on tiptoes
Roll to the left
Circle long tail in front of the body

The Piper
Skip forward left 2 steps
Skip forward right 2 steps
Circle anticlockwise 4 steps

Musical Journey

INTRODUCING THE INSTRUMENTS

Brass

The **trombone** is made from a long metal tube. At one end the tube opens into a bell shape. Part of the coiled tube forms a slide, which moves to form different notes. There is a mouthpiece, which is blown into.

The **trumpet** is made from a tightly coiled metal tube. It has a mouthpiece, which is blown into, at one end and a cone-shaped bell at the other.

Wind

The **flute** is a long, thin instrument, originally made of wood but now usually metal. The player blows across (not into) the blowhole at the mouthpiece. A metal cap (key) covers each finger hole. The keys are depressed to form different notes.

The **saxophone** is made of metal, but it is a wind instrument because it has a reed fixed into the mouthpiece. The reed vibrates to form sound. There are metal keys, which open and close holes to make notes. The bell end faces upwards and outwards.

Percussion

The **drum** is a circular instrument covered in a skin. Sounds are made when the skin is struck with drumsticks. The skin can be tightened to alter the pitch of the notes.

The **marimba** is an African xylophone, which stands at waist height. Sticks strike the series of wooden keys.

Keyboard

The **piano** has a series of keys which cause hammers to hit metal strings; the strings vibrate to produce sound. There are also foot pedals to control the volume.

Strings

The **cello** is a large, hollow, wooden instrument, which has four strings running its length. A bow is drawn across the strings to produce sound. Fingers pressing on strings increase the number of notes available. The instrument is held vertically.

The **violin** is similar to the cello but much smaller. It is held under the chin.

WARM-UP

Size and shape:

● Begin with small curled-up shapes growing slowly into large, wide/tall shapes. Use every part of the body.

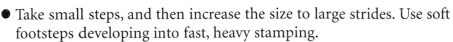

- Take small steps, and then increase the size to large strides. Use soft footsteps developing into fast, heavy stamping.
- Trace the shapes of instruments on the floor.

THE INSTRUMENTS

Talk about the instruments which make up an orchestra. Categorize them into sections, i.e. strings, wind, brass and percussion. Discuss the different sizes and shapes of instruments, the materials they are made of, and the variations in the way they are played. Write this on a board and include a picture if possible.

There are nine solo instruments on the CD. Introduce them one at a time (the order is not important). It is possible for every group to experience every instrument, although it works just as well to select groups to be certain instruments or even to allow pupils a choice of instrument (e.g. one instrument from each section).

With the first instrument, it is a good idea to choose a group of children and place them in position, allowing the class to suggest how to make the instrument look realistic.

Ask the pupils to imagine they are playing a **trombone**. Hold one hand to the mouth while the other hand moves the hand slide forwards and backwards.

Divide the class into groups of five or six. Line up three children, one behind the other, to show the movement of the hand slide. They should lunge forward, together, with the right leg and then slide it back along the floor to the starting position.

One pupil can be the mouthpiece, standing adjacent to the first person in the hand-slide line. He or she should bend knees and outstretch arms to illustrate that air is being blown into the instrument.

Two pupils may form the bell section, situated next to the last person in the hand-slide line. They should form a circular, bell shape and shake to illustrate sound coming out.

PROGRESSION

When the pupils are happy that their formation depicts a trombone, they can experiment with different ways of making the hand slide, the mouthpiece and bell section move. Suggest that they swap roles to experience different movements. Working in teams, using a count of 8, they can develop a group motif using all parts of the instrument.

2a Composition within small groups.

Give each group the opportunity to perform the motif to the class. This is a good way of sharing ideas.

Introduce another brass instrument, the **trumpet**. How does this instrument differ in size, shape and the way it is played? (Instead of the hand slide, the trumpet has three small buttons called valves, which are pressed down to make notes.) Encourage each group to experiment initially with the size and shape of the trumpet and then to develop a motif to illustrate it being played.

DIFFERENTIATION

Encourage pupils, working as a team, to develop their own ideas of how to illustrate the shape of an instrument. Some may be happy to experiment with complex movement patterns in groups, while others may wish to concentrate on basic patterns.

DEVELOPMENT

Begin to introduce the other instruments in the same way. The group sizes and dynamics may change throughout this process; for instance, smaller instruments may require fewer pupils. The important thing is to achieve quality of movement, so it may take a number of sessions to develop motifs for nine instruments.

The **flute** has lots of keys, so groups may arrange themselves spaced out in a line, with one person for the mouthpiece. Scrunching movements up and down would be best. The mouthpiece could move as if responding to a breeze.

With the **saxophone**, focus on the vibration of the mouthpiece, the pressing of the keys and the shaking of the upward facing bell.

The **marimba** requires members of the group to stand side by side, moving only when struck. Find different ways to show low notes at one end and high notes at the other.

Encourage groups to focus on the circular shape of the **drum** and the vibration of each strike of the drumsticks.

For the **piano**, pupils may choose to focus simply on the keys, low to high notes, or to illustrate the complexities of the piano.

Emphasis should be on drawing the bow upward and downward across the small shape for the **violin**. The larger size of the **cello** needs to be shown, and, as the bow is larger than the violin's, two or three pupils could join to draw the bow from side to side.

For each instrument, groups need to find the right balance to demonstrate the instrument, and then practise and perfect a motif to illustrate playing it. Some groups may wish to develop more instruments than others.

1a Consolidate existing skills and gain new ones.

1b Perform actions and skills with more consistent quality and control.

6b Respond to a range of stimuli and accompaniment.

6a Create and perform dances using a range of movement patterns.

Musical Journey

WARM-UP

Hard and soft:

- Walk, tiptoe, jog, side-step, stride and lunge around the room.
- When the music stops, hold a series of balances: hard, sharp and angular, and soft, rounded shapes.

INSTRUMENT MOTIFS

1b Perform actions and skills with more consistent control and quality.

Encourage each group to form a balance to demonstrate their favourite instrument. Let each group perform in turn so that the pupils are aware of how dramatic their instruments look.

6b Use movement imaginatively in response to musical stimulus.

Listen to the CD. When each solo instrument is played the group that has chosen that instrument performs its motif. When the motif is completed twice, the instrument balance is resumed. There are nine solo instruments, so while one instrument performs the others are waiting, just as in an orchestra. (Note that some children may be performing as more than one instrument.)

You will need to ensure that groups recognise their instrument on the CD and begin and finish at the correct time. The aim is to have a smooth transition between instruments.

PROGRESSION

2a Plan, use and adapt compositional ideas for small groups.

The next phase of the orchestra is where the instruments play in their sections. Make the children aware of which section their instrument belongs to. Listen to the CD together and identify the instruments and the sections in which they are playing. Groups may use the same motif or may decide to modify the original for the section playing. Allow the groups time to practise, alter and perfect this motif (which is performed twice).

DIFFERENTIATION

Some groups may have several **instrument motifs** to remember, and some children may belong to different groups. Others may have just one instrument motif to perfect. Give all groups time to achieve quality.

DEVELOPMENT

2b Develop and use knowledge of principles behind ideas to improve their effectiveness.
3a/b Identify what makes a performance effective. Suggest improvements based on this information.

Divide the class into two, then divide each group into the sections of the orchestra. Encourage one instrument to perform for another. The group that is watching should look for originality, presentation, timing and quality and try to suggest ways that the performance may be improved. The groups should then swap roles.

When both groups are happy with their performances they can continue working on each section with a better understanding of how the other instrument is performing. The exercise may reveal ways in which both **instrument motifs** are better able to complement each other.

Musical Journey

WARM-UP

Fast and slow:

- Wake up each body part individually, starting with small slow movements and gradually increasing in size and speed.
- Move across the room from one side to another. Begin with slow, small steps, increasing in size and speed.

THE ORCHESTRA

Start by revising the solo **instrument motifs**, in groups, using the CD. When the pupils are confident, move into the **sections phase** of the piece.

Arrange the instrument groups around the room as if in an orchestra. Establish a front of stage and focal point of the audience. Ask the pupils to create their instrument shapes (balances) in their orchestral positions. Check that there are a variety of shapes – tall, short, wide and thin – and that all instruments are recognizable. Take a photograph to show the class.

Use the CD to bring the solo instruments to life, followed by the various sections of the orchestra. The transition between the instruments should be smooth and when the instruments are not in use they should remain still in their balances.

1a Consolidate existing skills and gain new ones.

PROGRESSION: THE FINALE

This is when all the instruments combine to create the intense pinnacle of the piece with all its energy and emotion. Let the children listen to the finale on the CD, identify their instrument and have time to adapt their existing motif or create a new one to reflect the music.

2b Develop and use knowledge of the principles behind the ideas to improve their effectiveness.
6a/b Create and perform dances using a range of patterns. Respond to a range of stimuli and accompaniment.

Encourage the pupils to discuss possibilities within instrument groups and then practise, perfect and perform a **finale phrase**.

At various times during the orchestral finale, percussion instruments such as whistles will feature. Randomly choose individuals to make a quick percussion movement, then slip back into their movement group.

2c Apply rules for different activities (structured/creative).

The piece culminates in three distinct notes, which should be performed with great passion. This is then followed by a finishing position of all instrument balances. It may be the same or different from the starting balances. Encourage the pupils to decide. It is important that the visual image of the orchestra is strong at the end.

DIFFERENTIATION

Some groups will concentrate on one instrument and perform the same motif repeatedly. Others may form different instruments, and even different instrument groups, with an array of motifs throughout the finale.

Musical Structure

Solo: (00 – 1min. 49sec.)

Each instrument is introduced:

trombone

trumpet

piano

violin

cello

flute

saxophone

marimba

drum

Sections: (1min. 50sec. – 2min. 53sec.)

brass

keyboard

strings

wind

percussion

Finale: (2min. 54sec. – 4min. 18sec.)

All instruments playing together

Individual percussion accompaniments

The Sea

Brainstorm ideas about the shape and movements of the sea, e.g. forwards, backwards, circular motion, curling, swirling, sweeping, dragging.

WARM-UP
- Move in a space. Begin with straight lines, changing direction.
- Introduce travel in curved lines and then shapes.
- Draw the pupils' initials and let them make those shapes.
- Start with light, quiet, soft footsteps and build to heavier, faster ones.

THE MOVEMENT OF THE SEA
Experiment with various step patterns, walking to represent calm waters:
Forward 2; right 2; left 2; back 2. Forward 1; back 1; right 1; left 1.
Encourage pupils to join small groups and develop their own step patterns to express how the sea moves.

Explain that the motion of the sea is not simply backwards and forwards but more likely as follows:
Forward 2; diagonal back left 2; forward 2; diagonal back left 2.

2a Plan, use and adapt compositional ideas within small groups.

PROGRESSION
Organise the pupils in lines (like waves), holding hands. Try out the step pattern. What do they notice? As all movements are to the left, they quickly run out of space. This would happen to sand on a beach if groynes were not used to stop the sand moving. Describe longshore drift – the process where beach material is moved along the coast as a result of this movement.

To illustrate the movement in dance, and make use of the space, try:
Forward 2; diagonal back right 2; forward 2; diagonal back right 2.

DIFFERENTIATION
Begin the step pattern very slowly, and speed up only when everyone can follow. Encourage the pupils to call out the steps to help familiarize themselves with the pattern. Some pupils may be happy to experiment with more complex patterns in groups.

6a Create and perform dances using a range of movement patterns.

THE SEA DANCE
Divide the group into four lines. All pupils will complete the first phrase, after which the front line will lead off to their left. They must form a new line at the back. After the second phrase, the new front line peels off to the left to form a new line at the back. After four phrases the original group will be back at the front.

1b Perform actions and skills with more consistent quality and control.

DEVELOPMENT
Pupils work individually to develop steps to represent more stormy waters. They can include strides, lunges, leaps and skips. Again, encourage pupils to develop their own stormy step patterns.

1a Consolidate existing skills and gain new ones.
6b Respond to stimulus ('storm conditions').

The Sea

WARM-UP
- Begin with light, delicate movements, gently waking each part of the body.
- Make the movements larger and stronger.

SEA LIFE
Brainstorm types of sea life, and uses of the sea, e.g. birds, fish, plants, coral, fishing, oil rig, boats. As a class, explore the movements of the following, using the cue cards (page 62):

	Shape/Balance	Movement
Coral	sharp, rough, jagged, with holes	slow, fine, feathery
Seaweed	long, thin, soft, smooth	slimy, slippery, wriggling
Birds	outstretched wings, diving, flying, watching	gliding, swooping, soaring

Take each in turn or simply focus on one. Aim to find three shapes or balances to represent each, e.g. the activity of a sea bird:

Balance 1 – arms outstretched, straight neck, face up, one foot raised as in flight.
Balance 2 – arms above head, hands together, knees bent, ready to dive.
Balance 3 – curled up small, head on one side, waiting for prey.

Practise these balances (hold for three seconds).

PROGRESSION
When three balances have been learnt, join them together to form a sequence. The linking movements for the sea bird could be gliding, spinning or swooping.

DIFFERENTIATION
Some children may copy the teacher's idea and wish to work alone. Others may share ideas in a group and develop group balances.

DEVELOPMENT
Practise, perfect and perform the sequence. The first balance is a starting position and the last a finishing position. These are static and can convey a message to the audience.

1b Perform actions and skills with more consistent control and quality.

2a Compositional ideas for individual activities.

2b Develop and use knowledge of principles behind ideas to improve their effectiveness.

The Sea

WARM-UP
- Step patterns: straight, curved, circling, changing direction.
- Begin softly and slowly, then build up the strength and speed of movement.

THE SEA DANCE

With pupils in four lines, holding hands, begin the **Sea Phrase**. Use the CD as a guide. This is very effective as a class dance but can be performed in small groups to illustrate more complex step patterns.

6b Use movement imaginatively in response to musical stimulus.

Following the **Sea Phrase** there is **Movement Time** to enable pupils to find space or get into groups for their **Sea Life Phrase** (balances).

The music for the motif is less structured to enable the pupils to be more creative with their sequences. Each balance is held for three seconds and the final balance is held until the movement time begins.

2c Apply rules for different activities (structured/creative).

Use this movement time to return to the original four lines. The **Sea Phrase** is now repeated. The next movement time can be used to find a space.

THE FINALE

This section uses improvisation. Decide on a final shape, e.g. a ship or a pier. One person makes a starting shape and then everyone in turn must add to the shape to form the final shape. Pupils can describe their individual shape and its part in the large shape. The focus is on the developing balance and so pupils can decide what movements they would like to be doing until it is their turn to join the balance, e.g. curl up like pebbles or wriggle like seaweed. Take time to enable the pupils to modify and improve their own shape and help others to improve theirs. (Keep in mind that the shape needs to be identifiable by the audience.) Hold the position completely still until the sound of gently lapping water ceases. This is a great photo opportunity!

3a/b Identify what makes a performance effective./Suggest improvements based on this information.

DIFFERENTIATION

Some pupils may want to be inverted or take the weight of other children. This must be done safely. Others may simply balance, with contact to another.

Musical structure/Notation

0 – 21sec.	**Introduction** **(Gentle lapping of water/seagulls)**
22sec. – min. 07sec.	**Sea phrase**
1min. 08sec. – 1min. 22sec.	**Movement time (Stormy seas)**
1min. 23sec. – 1min. 46sec.	**Sea life phrase**
1min. 47sec. – 2min. 00sec.	**Movement time (Stormy seas)**
2min. 01sec. – 2min. 46sec.	**Repeat Sea phrase**
2min. 47sec. – 3min. 03sec.	**Movement time**
3min. 04sec. – 3min. 30sec.	**Finale (Improvisation)**
	– Fade out … (Gentle lapping of water

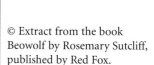

Beowulf: Dragonslayer   Phase 1

(Inspired by the book of this name by Rosemary Sutcliff)

AN EXTRACT FROM CHAPTER 6 THE SEA-HAG

© Extract from the book Beowolf by Rosemary Sutcliff, published by Red Fox.

Down and down sank Beowulf into the cold swinging depths; down and down for what seemed the whole of a day. From all sides the tusked sea beasts rushed in upon him, striving to gore him to pieces; and ever as he sank he fought them off with stroke and lunge of the great sword Hrunting. At last his feet touched the sea floor, and instantly an enemy far more dire was upon him, as the sea-hag leapt to fling her arms about him, clutching him to her with claws as terrible as her son's had been. He was being rushed through the black depths, close-locked in her dreadful embrace, and now, still together, they were diving upward through the under-water mouth of a cave.

Up and up… They were in a vast sea-hall above the tide line, white sand underfoot, and the faint light of day falling in shafts from some opening to the cliff top far above. Beowulf tore himself free and springing clear for a sword stroke, brought Hrunting whistling down on her head. The cave rang with the blow, but for the first time since it was forged the blade refused to bite, and next instant she was upon him once more. He stumbled beneath her onslaught and she flung him down with herself on top of him, stabbing again and again at his breast with her saex, her broad-bladed dagger, and when that failed to pierce his battle-sark, clawing and worrying at him as though she were a wolf indeed. He saw her fangs sharp behind her snarling lips, and her eyes shone with balefire amid the tangle of her hair; but the ring-mail of the Queen's gift withstood her still, and gathering his strength he flung her off a second time, and springing up, aimed at her a blow that should have swept her head from her shoulders.

There on the silver sand, with the roar of the sea echoing about them hollow like the echo in a vast shell, he with one arm locked about her and the other straining at her dagger wrist, she striving always with fang and claw to come at his heart, they reeled and trampled to and fro …

Long and bitter was the struggle, but there was a strength in the sea-hag that had not been in her son, and Beowulf could not overcome it. Some weapon he must have, and as he fought he snatched desperate glances about him in search of one. Here and there were ancient weapons hung on the rock walls of the cavern, and amongst them the light from the roof fell upon one sword, a huge sword, dwarf-wrought perhaps for giants in the far past days, for it was so long in the blade and broad in the grip that no man save Beowulf could have wielded it. Seeing it, his heart leapt up with fresh hope, and gathering all his strength and cunning he gave way before the sea-hag's onslaught, then swerved and sprang sideways past her, to snatch it from the wall. His hand closed over the hilt, and with a triumphant battle-shout he whirled around and brought the blade down upon her in a flashing swoop of fire.

It shored through hair and hide and bone, and Grendel's Dam dropped without a sound, her hideous head all but smitten from her shoulders.

WARM-UP

● Encourage pupils as individuals to embark on a journey. Rowing a boat, which then sinks. Swimming for shore. Running up a hot sandy beach.

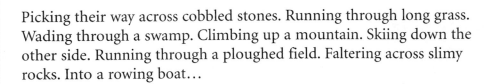

Picking their way across cobbled stones. Running through long grass. Wading through a swamp. Climbing up a mountain. Skiing down the other side. Running through a ploughed field. Faltering across slimy rocks. Into a rowing boat…

There are two very different characters in the passage. Dance drama is an ideal medium with which to illustrate these differences and the fight scene will excite both boys and girls. Study each of the characters separately so that all pupils understand each role. This will improve the interaction when they perform as a pair.

BEOWULF

He is clad in his ring-mail sark (shirt), his boar-crested helmet pulled low upon his brow, his sword in hand. Brainstorm words that could be used to describe Beowulf, e.g. strong, proud, determined, confident. What types of movement would best illustrate this character? Consider upright, controlled, athletic, precise movements.

Teach the **Beowulf starting motif** to the whole class.
1. Starting position tall, strong, with sword aloft.
2. Jump up as if diving.
3. 180 degree turn to crouch on the floor.
4. Hold crouch position on floor.
5. Spring up with arms raised.
6. Slowly pull arms down to sides (breaststroke).
7. Put left hand across face for protection.
8. Sweep right hand across body to fight away sea beasts.
9. Wide leg stance, knees bent, with fists raised.

1b Perform actions and skills with more consistent control and quality.

Pupils should practise in pairs/threes, marking through the motif and perfecting the timing. Suggestions can be made on how to improve the motif.

Divide the class in half, enabling pupils to perform for each other and to illustrate the effectiveness of this opening phase.

THE SEA-HAG

A monstrous, evil 'wolf-woman of the sea', she is described as having claws and fangs, with long snaky hair. She was armed with a dagger and had superior strength. She was 'Death-Shadow-in-the-Dark', mad with grief at the loss of her beloved son.

Discuss how anger and revenge made the sea-hag both physically and mentally strong. The description of 'wolf-woman' indicates that her strength is greater than a man's, more like that of a wild animal. Similarly, her movements will be more wild, out of control and thunderous.

Teach the **Sea-hag starting motif** to the whole class.
1. Starting position crouched low, with hands/arms covering face.
2. Using a count of 8, slowly uncurl using jagged, sharp, angular movements.

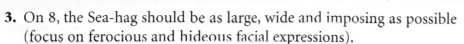

3. On 8, the Sea-hag should be as large, wide and imposing as possible (focus on ferocious and hideous facial expressions).

4. The Sea-hag is now ready to pounce!

This is a freer and more expressive type of movement than that of Beowulf. Encourage pupils to be as wild as possible with their ideas, and to try various ways of growing to their full, menacing height. They should try to illustrate her huge, cumbersome frame with her desperate, flailing arms and slow, gnarling movements.

Again, divide the class into two to share ideas and improve presentation skills.

PROGRESSION

In pairs, each pupil should experiment with both roles. Allow them to decide who will play each character in their finished performance.

Using a count of 8, they should perform both motifs at the same time co-operatively. Encourage the pupils to count for themselves.

Pay particular attention to strong, clear, starting positions, followed by large, obvious motif movements. Emphasize the need to identify each role clearly from the beginning.

DIFFERENTIATION

Some Sea-hag pupils may wish to experiment with moving silently around Beowulf as he/she performs the **Beowulf starting motif**, at the same time as uncurling. This will give the impression of hiding and stalking the prey. Other pupils may prefer to focus on uncurling slowly and independently on the spot.

DEVELOPMENT

The loud crash following the count of 8 indicates the first point of contact between Beowulf and the Sea-hag. As a pair, pupils should decide on a dramatic first clash, e.g. the Sea-hag pounces forward, grabbing Beowulf with both fists, or attacks from behind, pulling Beowulf's shoulders backwards. This should be a choreographed 'clash', in which both partners know what is going to happen. The focus is on safety and control.

Let them experiment with a variety of 'clashes', each one to be held perfectly still for three seconds. Variations may be the level or direction of attack by the Sea-hag, and/or the intensity of the pupils' facial expressions. Emphasize the need for good body tension to hold strong, angular shapes completely still.

Pupils should decide on the 'clash' with the best visual impact, practise and perfect it. In pairs, they should practise and perform the starting phrases culminating in the 'clash'. Use the CD to dictate the timing.

The contrast between the structured movement of Beowulf and the more expressive movements of the Sea-hag can be very effective. Give the pupils an opportunity to perform this phrase, and share good ideas with the class.

2c Apply rules and conventions for different activities.

2a Plan, use and adapt strategies, tactics and compositional ideas for pairs.

1a Consolidate existing skills and gain new ones

1b Perform actions and skills with more consistent control and quality.

6a Create and perform dances using a range of movement patterns.

Beowulf: Dragonslayer   Phase 2

WARM-UP
- Soldiers marching on spot, then moving forwards and backwards.
- Military drill exercises. Look left and right with the head, as if on watch. Salute with left arm, circle it backwards, followed by the right.
- March to various points in the room and stretch specific muscles, e.g. abdominal, upper and lower legs, in each place.

There are two phases of combat to investigate:
- The sweeping and jabbing of swords and daggers.
- Pushing and pulling/lifting and throwing in unarmed combat.

SWORDS/DAGGERS
Discuss the types of movement made with a sword. For example, sweeping, scything, flowing, gliding, stretching, precise and graceful movements. Discuss the types of movement made with a dagger. For example, plunging, jabbing, thrusting, stabbing, short, sharp and explosive movements.

1b Perform actions and skills with more consistent control and quality.

Let the pupils work in pairs, in character, to practise a selection of movements illustrating the use of both the sword and the dagger. They should exaggerate the sweeping movements, fully extending the arm and making large circling motions, and similarly, enlarge the stabbing motion of the dagger to emphasize its strength and power.

1a Consolidate existing skills and gain new ones.

Encourage each pair to work together as if in a fight. When one of them is on the attack, the other must react to that approach using defensive movements. Talk about the types of movement needed to avoid the blade of a sword or the stab of a dagger, e.g. falling backwards to the floor. In dance no real contact is made. The blows must look realistic but should not actually make contact.

PROGRESSION

2a/b Plan, use and adapt compositional ideas for pairs or small groups./Develop and use their knowledge of the principles behind ideas to improve performance.

Using the 'clash' balance as a starting position, develop a phrase composed of various **sword/dagger** attacks and reactions. Pupils should link movements by rolling on the floor, spinning to change direction, or leaping as if to pounce. This is a creative piece with no set number of movements/motifs. Use the CD (42sec. – 1min 15sec.), to determine the length of this phase of the tussle. Practise to establish clearly choreographed routines, thus improving the authenticity of the fight and ensuring safety.

DIFFERENTIATION
Some children may be overenthusiastic and determined to fight too realistically. Be sure to restrict the number of attacks and responses for those children. Control is vital and will have a great effect on the visual impact of the dance. Some pairs will require no limitations and their creativity will need no boundaries.

Musical Structure

0 – 15sec.	Introduction
16 – 33sec.	Starting motif (8 count)
34 – 41sec.	Clash (3 sec.)
42sec. – 1min. 15sec.	Swords/daggers
1min. 16sec. – 1min. 53sec.	Push and pull
(1min. 42sec. – 1min. 53sec.	Lift and throw)
1min. 54sec. – 2min. 02sec.	Clash (3 sec.)
2min. 03sec. – 3min. 23sec.	Final phrase Final sweep of the sword Plunge of death Victorious finale

(Inspired by the book
of this name by
Antoine de
Saint-Exupéry)

The Little Prince

Phase 1

WARM-UP

- A journey in a light aircraft: Arm circles to start the rotary blades, hip rotations to start the engine, high knee lifts, as the pistons grow faster.
- In the air, lots of turbulence, bumping up and down, circular movement patterns, leaping up on thermals, slumping down through the clouds… spinning out of control, lower, and closer and closer to the floor, until crash landing in a heap.

Introduce the book *The Little Prince*. Explain the story, using extracts to set the scene.

A pilot forced to land in the Sahara meets a little prince. The little prince tells wise and enchanting stories about his own tiny planet with three volcanoes, uncontrollable baobab plants, beautiful sunsets and a single haughty flower.

Each day, the little prince goes about his daily routine of raking out his active volcanoes. This is to stop them erupting, and so that they regularly warm his breakfast. He also rakes the extinct volcano, just in case!
He regularly uproots Baobab shoots before they take hold. He has to be disciplined about this, as these bad seeds can develop into plants, which grow taller than churches.
One of his great pleasures is to sit and enjoy watching the sunset.
His planet boasts one simple flower, a single rose. He tends, waters and shelters this flower, which perfumes his planet and lights up his life.
Time spent nurturing and protecting the rose makes the rose important, it is tamed.

Ask the pupils to imagine what life would be like if they were the little prince living alone on a planet the size of a house. The little prince loved sunsets. On our large planet we see the sun set once a day, but we would have to travel many miles across time zones to see it set again on the same day. However, by moving his chair a little, the little prince was able to see the sun set many times. On one day he saw 44 sunsets!

A possible **sunset motif** might be:
(a) ● With weight on left foot, face the front right-hand corner of the room.
  - Place your right foot in front of your left, pointing to the same corner.
  - Look to the sky, with your right hand shielding your eyes from the sun.
  - Place your left hand behind your back.

Rotate the motif, moving it to face the remaining three corners of the room:
(b) ● Transfer weight to the right foot, and move the left leg around the right one (270 degrees), until it is facing the back right-hand corner of the room.
  - Stand facing the back right-hand corner of the room.
  - Look to the sky, with the left hand shielding the eyes.
  - The right hand should be placed behind the back.

Transfer weight to the left foot, and move the right foot sideways and forwards, until it is facing the back left-hand corner of the room. Repeat (a), facing the back left-hand corner of the room.

Repeat (b) so that everyone returns to the starting point, facing the front right-hand corner of the room.

Encourage the pupils to practise in pairs to perfect the motif and iron out any problems. Use the CD to develop the timing.

PROGRESSION

In groups, pupils should choose to explore either the baobab trees, the rose or raking the volcanoes.

Baobabs
Tall, strong, thick branches, entwined, twisted, angular movements. Use cue cards as prompts (page 63).

The rose
It develops from a shoot, petals open out, and then open and shut with day and night. Variations may include movements caused by the wind or visiting caterpillars. Use the flower cue cards as prompts (page 63).

Volcanoes
● raking action
● sparky movements of active volcanoes
A group may wish to divide roles, e.g. three individuals may develop movements to illustrate the bubbling of lava, while another may provide the raking movements. Use the volcano cue cards to stimulate ideas (page 64).

DIFFERENTIATION

Some children may prefer to perfect the **sunset motif** and then modify it to develop a phrase rather than choosing a completely new area of movement. Others may prefer to choose more than one of the themes, and work towards smoothly linking phrases together.

DEVELOPMENT

There is a great deal of material in this phase. There are several ways in which you could approach its delivery.
● Concentrate on just one out of the three topics and investigate this thoroughly. Focus on an initial motif and explore its development.
● There are three clear styles: abstract (baobabs); structured (rose); dance drama (volcano). Enable the children to choose a topic. This may provide greater creativity and ownership.
● Explore all three areas in brief. Tackle each topic on an improvisation basis, i.e. a quick, unplanned response to each theme.
● It is possible to explore all three areas in detail but this would require several lessons.

1a Consolidate existing skills and gain new ones.

1b Perform actions and skills with more consistent control and quality.

2a Plan, use and adapt strategies, tactics and compositional ideas for pairs or small groups.
6b Respond to a range of stimuli.

1b Perform actions and skills with more consistent control and quality.
6a Create and perform dances using a range of movement patterns.
2c Apply rules and conventions for different activities.

The Little Prince

WARM-UP

- Static stretches starting from the head and working down. Emphasize stretching; tall, thin, and wide.

Revise the **sunset motif** and **group phrases**. Initially mark them through with no accompaniment and then introduce the music.

While on his travels to other planets the little prince meets various inspirational characters, not least on Earth, where a fox teaches him that you become responsible for what you have tamed. The fox shows him that an individual sees clearly with the heart, and that "anything essential is invisible to the eyes". He illustrates the importance of care, trust, support, mutual respect and loyalty.

This section relates to the wise words of the fox. Organize the pupils in pairs and explain that in order for partner balance to be effective there must be trust/co-operation. Highlight the importance of safety.

A balance is a shape or position which is held completely still for three seconds. Encourage pupils to use one or more points of contact for their partner balance. Initiate work by suggesting hands, feet, head, elbows, etc. Challenge pairs to find as many different points of contact as possible and as many balances. Give frequent opportunities to share ideas.

2a Plan, use and adapt compositional ideas for pairs

Highlight interesting examples and suggest that everyone make an attempt at them. While all doing the same balance, ask pupils to make one change to make the balance different. Highlight the variations.

Partner balance can be explored through the following five areas:
- symmetrical balances – (mirroring);
- push and pull balances – (symmetrical/asymmetrical);
- asymmetrical balances – (one high/one low or thin/wide);
- taking weight – (one partner lifted off the floor by the other);
- inversion – (one or both partners balanced upside down).

1a Consolidate existing skills and gain new ones.

By exploring each of these areas individually, pupils will have the opportunity to develop complex, well-thought-out balances. Emphasize the idea that subtle modifications can create very striking effects.

PROGRESSION

1b Perform actions and skills with more consistent control and quality.

The pupils should now be equipped with a large vocabulary of balances and are subsequently in a position to choose their favourite/most aesthetically pleasing. Encourage each pair to choose their favourite/best five balance positions. They should practise and demonstrate them in isolation.

Develop a sequence of five balances. Ask the pupils to think about ways in which the balances could be smoothly linked. Suggest the use of spins, rolls, jumps, strides and stretches instead of walking or shuttling between balances. Explain that it is part of the choreography and viewed by the audience in the same way as the balances. Any fussing detracts from the balances and appears unstructured or rushed.

2a/b Plan, use and adapt compositional ideas for pairs or small groups./Develop and use their knowledge of the principles behind ideas to improve performance.

DIFFERENTIATION

Some pupils may feel confident enough to do radical and complicated balances. Encourage this, but emphasize safety for both partners. Others may prefer to work towards basic, teacher-led balances. Similarly, some children will have the confidence to explore balances in all five areas, while others may do better if they concentrate on balances in one or two areas. Explain that simple balances are often the most effective.

DEVELOPMENT

Use the CD to identify the delicate phase of the music (2min. 01sec. – 3min. 23sec.).
Perform the sequences with accompaniment. The rhythm is calm and relaxed, which should encourage the children to move slowly and smoothly. Encourage them to think about how the audience will view the performance, and consider the use of space, changes in level and variation in shape throughout the sequence.

6a/b Create and perform dances using a range of movement patterns./Respond to a range of stimuli and accompaniment.

Ask each pair to join up with another pair to decide what makes a good performance. Encourage groups to discuss quality and how to achieve it. Ask them to decide what they like/dislike about the sequence and suggest ways in which it might be improved. They should work on presentation skills such as timing, linking and stillness.

3a/b Identify what makes a performance effective./Suggest improvements based on this information.

Blue

(Inspired by *Rhapsody in Blue* by George Gershwin)

WHAT DOES 'BLUE' MEAN TO YOU?

Brainstorm ideas and thoughts about what blue means to the children. Write or draw the ideas on paper/the board in categories. Remember that some may not fit neatly into any one group. Ideas might include:

Objects: primary colour, deep blue sea, sky, cobalt, bluebird, blue peter flag, bluebell, bluebottle fly, blueprint – plan for work, Chelsea FC, the band Blue.
Sayings: blue blood – royal, out of the blue – unexpected, blue in the face – angry, blue with the cold.
Feelings: feeling low, sad, depressed, and empty.

Label three envelopes with the category headings: 'Objects', 'Sayings' and 'Feelings and Emotions'. Photocopy the cue cards (pages 64–66) and collate the cards in three envelopes. Each envelope will then contain the sub category headings and a number of descriptors. Thus the 'Objects' envelope will have in it, 'The Sea', 'The Sky', 'Bluebell' and 'Chelsea FC' and their descriptors (e.g. 'Ebb and Flow', 'Glide', 'Seed', 'Kick' etc.)

Prepare three large sheets of blue card, with the categories as titles. Divide the pupils into three groups and give each group an envelope and the relevant sheet of card. Ask the children to group the descriptor cards into the appropriate sub categories, mount them on card and display them for the other groups. The sheets of card will then be used in the next Phases.

2c Apply rules and conventions for different activities.

WARM-UP
Static stretches:
- Begin with the head and very slowly stretch and wake each part of the body. Ask the children to imagine that their limbs are heavy and lifeless when they start to move, just as if they were feeling 'Blue'.
- Encourage the children to notice how movements change when they are done with more energy.

Draw everyone's attention to the Feelings and Emotions category.
Ask the children if they have ever felt 'blue'? What did it feel like? Can they describe it in words?

1b Perform actions and skills with more consistent control and quality.

Try to describe/illustrate those feelings with a motif, e.g. hang head; holding head in hands; crouch low; curl up and rock; cheek on fist; chin on inside of hands; curled up on floor; slow movements/steps; scuff feet; drooped shoulders.

1a Consolidate existing skills and gain new ones.

In pairs, encourage the children to experiment with 'blue' motifs, imagining that they feel sad about something! Pick out some good ideas and/or ask a few children to share their ideas to increase the impetus.

PROGRESSION

The aim is to develop a phrase based on three motifs, designed to convey sadness. Each pair can either choose their favourite motifs and try to link them, or build a phrase by developing / expanding one motif.

Note: Linkages should be slow and deliberate to illustrate the low energy nature of depression.

DIFFERENTIATION

Some children may need to act out a familiar scenario, e.g. when their football team concedes a goal, to enable them to exhibit their emotions. Initially allow them to scream / howl, then tell them to experience the same feelings without volume! Others will be able to draw upon their experience to illustrate isolated symbols of emotion.

DEVELOPMENT

Using the first 30 sec. of the 'Blue' section of the CD, establish a starting position depicting the mood. Develop the phrase in unison (together) or by moving separately to illustrate that there may be conflict between the pair. Decide on a finishing position, illustrating feelings of hopelessness and sadness. Some pairs may repeat the original phrase several times to illustrate boredom and monotony, others may prefer to modify the original phrase to incorporate more ideas of sadness and feeling low.

1a Consolidate existing skills and gain new ones.
2a Plan, use and adapt strategies, tactics and compositional ideas for pairs.

1b Perform actions and skills with more consistent control and quality.
6a Create and perform dances using a range of movement patterns.

Blue

WARM-UP

- Small, scrunched shapes in contrast with large, stretched shapes.
- Use one of each of these types of movement for each body part, starting from the top, and working down.
- Move in space around the room, using both small, quiet, sad footsteps and large, loud, confident strides.
- Revisit the **'feelings' phrase** of the **Blue** dance.

The next phase of the music runs from 30 sec. to 1min 50 sec. and investigates 'objects' which are **blue** in colour.

Use the 'objects' list displayed on the wall as a stimulus. Ask the children if they can think of any others?

Organise the class in pairs or small groups (they can be different from the 'feelings' groups). Encourage each group to decide on a blue object and explore how that object might move. E.g. a bluebell begins as a seed, opens out, shoots up, its petals open and it blows in the wind. The petals continuously open and close before they fall off as the stem withers and sinks to the ground.

Note: Explore the development of a bluebell as a class to stimulate movement ideas but be sure to allow children to use their own objects and creativity if they desire. Allow groups time to fully explore their theme, give them opportunities to share ideas and perform for others.

PROGRESSION

Encourage each group to develop a phrase of movements which illustrate their chosen object. Practise, perfect and perform the sequence until they are confident enough to perform to others. Focus on making the movements and message clear enough for others to guess the object.

DIFFERENTIATION

Some pupils may be able to work independently following the teacher's idea and guidance, others may wish to completely initiate and develop a theme on their own.

DEVELOPMENT

Using the CD (30 sec. – 1 min. 50 sec.), encourage the pupils either to repeat their phrase or to expand and modify it to fit the music. There should be a distinct start and finish to this phase of the music.

Discuss quality and how to achieve it. Ask the pupils what makes a good performance. They should work on presentation skills such as timing, linking and emphasizing their movements.

2a/b Plan, use and adapt compositional ideas for pairs or small groups./Develop and use their knowledge of the principles behind the ideas to improve performance.

1b Perform actions and skills with more consistent control and quality.

6b Respond to a range of stimuli and accompaniment.

3a/b Identify what makes a performance effective./ Suggest improvements based on this information.

Blue

WARM-UP

- Begin with light, delicate movements, gently waking each part of the body.
- Make the movements larger and stronger.
- Revisit the **'objects' phrase** of the **Blue** dance.

Brainstorm the sayings associated with blue. Discuss their meanings. Explore some movement ideas for each and suggest ways of linking these movements together, e.g. 'blue with cold':

- Wrapping arms around the body (hugging);
- Patting hands against arms while in that position;
- Wrapping and unwrapping arms (exaggerate this and make it really large).

In groups of three or four, ask the children to select a saying and experiment with motifs to develop a phrase.

6a Create and perform dances using a range of movement patterns.

PROGRESSION

Encourage one pupil in each group to watch the other members of the group. Ask them to decide what they like/dislike about the phrase and suggest ways in which it might be improved. Swap roles so that everyone has a chance to observe.

3a/b Identify what makes a performance effective./Suggest improvements based on this information.

DIFFERENTIATION

The more able pupils may wish to explore several sayings within this section. It is essential that these link smoothly together and that they provide strong enough imagery to stand out. Equally, one short repeated phrase which has been practised and perfected would have a visually strong impact.

DEVELOPMENT

This section of the CD runs from 1 min. 50 sec. to 2 min. 40 sec. Encourage the pupils to develop a start, middle and finish which lasts for the entire 50 seconds.

2b Develop and use their knowledge of the principles behind the ideas to improve their effectiveness.

The music for **Blue** is less structured to enable pupils to be more creative with their sequences. However, there should be a formal start and finish position to add clarity to the phrase.

2c Apply rules for different activities (structured/creative).

Give each group an opportunity to perform with the music for the rest of the class.

6a/b Create and perform dances using a range of movement patterns./ Respond to a range of stimuli.

Blue

THE PERFORMANCE

It is not essential to use the fourth phase of this dance instruction because all three elements of Blue can be taught as stand-alone topics, or linked simply using the first 2 min. 40 sec. of this section of the CD. However, there is a performance element written into this theme which deals with all the complexities of Blue in a class or large group perspective.

Note: Pupils need to get to know the music and be able to recognize the start and finish of each phase. This will ensure the smooth flow of the dance performance.

GROUP ORGANIZATION

All pupils may perform the whole dance at the same time. The class can be divided into as many groups as required and distributed sensitively so that all children can be seen.

Each group may choose their favourite phrase from the three sections and solely perform that, holding a silent, still position while other groups perform their phrases. The use of stillness and frozen finishing positions helps the audience to focus on the group which is moving. Pupils may wish to sink to low, curled positions on the floor when not performing, and then rise when they perform again. This may need to be reflected in changes to the starting and finishing positions in order to make the movement flow.

The final two phases, Objects(2) and Feelings(2), are of a different length compared to the original Objects and Feelings sections, (see Musical structure, page 53). This means that modifications need to be made to fit the music in those sections. This enables different groups to feature in different phases, but also gives the opportunity to develop a spectacular whole group ending.

You could either video the performance or divide the class so that the pupils can watch each other perform. Encourage them to observe performance skills and the overall impression of the dance. Ask them to comment on the use of space and different levels (e.g. pupils working at high and low levels), also formation (e.g. positioned in straight lines, circles or different shapes). Encourage the pupils to alter their shape/movements in order to improve the overall aesthetic appearance of the performance.

Musical structure

00 – 30sec.	Feelings	(30 sec.)
30sec. – 1min. 50sec.	Objects	(1min. 10 sec.)
1min. 50sec. – 2min. 40sec.	Sayings	(50 sec.)
2min. 40sec. – 3min. 18sec.	Objects (2)	(38 sec.)
3min. 18sec. – 3min. 48sec.	Feelings (2)	(30 sec.)

African Dance

(Based on the rhythms and dance of the Adzohu, or Fon Ewe people, of West Africa)

WARM-UP

- Begin with hand claps to initiate a basic rhythm.
- Introduce other body parts, e.g. move hips, punch arms and flap elbows. Ask pupils to suggest other body parts.
- Try variations of the rhythm, making it more complex.
- Stamp feet to the rhythm. Vary the intensity (hard and soft).
- Move around the room: stamp, stamp, jump or stamp, hop, jump. Vary the direction of the step/jump and also the level, e.g. low lunges, high hops, quick side steps and a jump backwards.
- Make up some rhythms and encourage the pupils to make up their own. Change pace, e.g. fast, slow, slow, fast.

Introduce the Fon Ewe people of West Africa. Describe how all members of the community join together in movement to illustrate their strength as a 'family' and a unit. African drumming and movement are used to tell a story or illustrate feelings. This dance piece investigates the strength and power of a group whose common aim is to work together for the good of the community.

Ask pupils to imagine the class being an African people. There are differences between all of its members: gender, height, age, strengths, weaknesses and interests. However, the group functions effectively by giving each individual a voice and a role in the community. There are individual tasks, partner tasks and group activities, which operate over time to make a successful people.

Use a drum or clap to introduce the basic rhythm for the first phase of the dance:
Bam Bam Bam (**Hard** Soft Soft)
Initially, ask the pupils to clap this beat. Ensure that they recognize the difference between hard and soft. When they are confident, encourage them to use their feet:

Stamp Step Step   **Left** Right Left   **Right** Left Right

Ask them to practise the rhythm with a partner, slowly at first, checking the change in intensity (hard and soft).

Show the pupils how they can change direction whilst keeping the same rhythm:
- Facing the front, lift the left knee and move it across the body.
- Step the left foot to the floor, facing the wall to your right (90-degree turn).
- Step the right foot to the floor.
The call for this motif can be: Lift. Step. Step.

Try the same motif moving in the opposite direction. Start by lifting the right leg and turning anticlockwise.

Again, ask the pupils to practise in pairs. Suggest that each one in turn observes the other, while clapping the rhythm, and makes comments which help to improve performance.

1a Consolidate existing skills and gain new ones.

1b Perform actions and skills with more consistent quality and control.

3a/b Identify what makes a performance effective./Suggest improvements based on this information.

PROGRESSION

With everyone facing the front, practise the **individual phrase** as a group.

Stamp Left	Step Right Step Left	Facing Front
Stamp Right	Step Left Step Right	
Stamp Left	Step Right Step Left	Facing Front
Stamp Right	Step Left Step Right	
Lift Left Turn	Step Left Step Right	90-degree turn
Stamp Right	Step Left Step Right	
Lift Left Turn	Step Left Step Right	90-degree turn (Facing Back)

Continue 90-degree turns until pupils are facing the front again. Repeat the motif left and right. Individuals may practise with a partner/group to perfect the timing of this phrase. Initially count slowly, working towards using the CD (11sec. – 37sec.).

6b Respond to a range of stimuli and accompaniment.

DIFFERENTIATION

Remember that you should also face the front when leading or the pupils may become confused. Similarly, when everyone is facing the back wall you may feel the need to move to continue leading. It is helpful to pair or group pupils who are struggling with those who have already picked it up. Keep changing the pairings until everyone is confident.

DEVELOPMENT

Encourage pairs to use the same rhythm but to modify or radically change the step pattern.

Suggestions for keeping the idea simple:
Stamp Heel Toe
Stamp Foot shuffle (count of 2).

More radical variations:
- Deep lunge left.
- Weight on left leg.
- Slide right foot across floor.
- Return to stand, feet together (count of 2).
Or
- Jump forwards.
- Lunge back left leg, drag back right.
- Return to standing (count of 2).

Allow pupils time to develop ideas. Encourage them to clap or count the rhythm and develop timing.

2a Composition within small groups.

Give each group the opportunity to perform the motif to the class. This is a good way of sharing ideas.

African Dance

WARM-UP

- Stretch all areas of the body, using a count of 4.
- Emphasize the rhythms, e.g. turning the head to warm up the neck:
  Turn the head to the left.
  Return to centre.
  Turn the head to the right.
  Return to centre.
  And:
  Lower chin to chest.
  Return to centre.
  Raise chin to ceiling.
  Return to centre.

FOLLOW MY LEADER

Encourage the pupils to choose a partner. Each pupil should have the chance to be a leader. Initially use a drum to define the rhythm. Encourage the leader to improvise, using any part of the body in the following ways:

- Hard beat – strong, powerful, heavy movements
- Soft beat – light, soft or quick movements

6a Create and perform dances using a range of movement patterns.

Use body part cue cards (page 68) to stimulate this task. Let each leader see the list of cue cards before leading their partner.

3a/b Identify what makes a performance effective./Suggest improvements based on this information.

Ask the others in each pair to mirror, or copy directly, the actions of the leader. Then let them swap roles. Give the pairs an opportunity to discuss which were their favourite movements and why.

PROGRESSION

1a/b Consolidate existing skills and gain new ones./Perform actions and skills with more consistent control and quality.

Encourage each pair to choose three of the most interesting motifs and link them together to form a **mirror phrase**. Practise the execution of each movement, concentrating on quality and timing. Suggest the children count out loud, or chant cue words when practising.

2a/b Plan, use and adapt compositional ideas in pairs./Develop and use their knowledge of the principles behind the ideas to improve their effectiveness.

Experiment with ways of linking movements, e.g. sliding, striding or jumping, remembering that all movements must be mirrored.

DEVELOPMENT

To make a phrase more interesting, suggest variations in level, e.g. working on the floor, on a high level or moving sideways. Similarly, ask children to consider changes in speed, e.g. combine fast movements with slower ones in the sequence.

6a Create and perform dances using a range of movement patterns.

Practise the phrase, working towards using the CD (56sec. – 1min. 48sec.).

African Dance

WARM-UP

- Begin walking as a group to all the corners of the room.
- Change to jogging, skipping, and hopping.
- Stop at each corner to stretch isolated body parts.
- Following each stretch announce a rhythm, e.g. hop, skip, jump, jump, which the children are required to do en route to the next corner.
- Change the stretches at each corner and the rhythm of travel to get to each corner.

Revise the **mirror phrase** in pairs. Label pupils A and B within each pair and ask pairs to join with another to make fours. A's should swap partners within the four, and work with a new B. A will become the leader and show their new partner their mirror phrase. B can join in and copy them when they feel confident. Swap over to let B's become leaders.

1a/b Consolidate existing skills and gain new ones./Perform actions with more consistent control and quality

TEACHING POINT

This will allow the spread of ideas, and also help groups function when they work as a unit of four.

The focus for the **group phrase** is opposites. Discuss as a class some opposite reactions to movements, e.g. low and high, wide and thin, hard and soft.

Within their groups of four, encourage the children to experiment with the idea of opposite movements. Use ideas from the mirror phrase or develop completely new motifs. Some new ideas may be better suited to groups of four.

To instigate activity, ask each group to think of a body part and/or type of movement, and instruct the group to their left to find opposite movements for this. Suggest the children demonstrate these ideas.

2a Plan, use and adapt compositional ideas for small groups.

Using the CD (1min. 49sec. – 2min. 31sec.), listen to the rhythm and try to identify the 8 counts:

1	2	psst	psst	5	6	7	8

Direct pupils to develop a **group phrase** which illustrates opposite reactions and lasts for a count of 8. This may be eight individual movements, or may be less, some movements taking two or more counts to complete, e.g. jumping to crouch low on the floor is 1 count, but to return to standing is 2. Beats 3 and 4 are a psst, psst sound. Children may like to do something special on those counts!

2b Develop and use knowledge of the principles behind the ideas to improve their effectiveness.

PROGRESSION

When the **group phrases** have been established, take time to consider the presentation. Suggest that subtle changes in formation and group structure can have a dramatic effect on the aesthetic appearance of the performance, e.g.

6a Create and perform dances using a range of movement patterns, including those from different cultures

working side by side or one behind the other. There could also be changes in the use of space, e.g. some groups will be static, while others choose to move in space and illustrate changes in direction.

DIFFERENTIATION

Group size may vary and exact pairs/fours may not be possible. Allow all pupils the opportunity to be leader and suggest ways in which mirroring in a triangle shape may look effective.

DEVELOPMENT

The **group phrase** is repeated eight times in total. However, after four times it is interrupted by a war cry (2min. 05sec. – 2min. 14sec.). Ask the pupils to listen to this phase of the music.

The sounds "wow uhh wow uhh" are quite striking. How does it make the pupils feel?
Suggest they move freely in space, leaping and landing in any way to express themselves as individuals. Encourage the children to use the sounds to shape their movements, as if a spirit controls their actions. Experiment with stillness. Hold a strong, powerful, menacing position. Experiment with facial expressions to increase the atmosphere.

2c Apply rules for different activities (structured/creative). 6b Respond to a range of stimuli and accompaniment.

Practise the **group phrase**, incorporating the war cry, with the music. Divide the class in half to perform this phrase, so that one half can observe the others. Ask the pupils to highlight the interesting areas and suggest changes to weak areas.

African Dance   *Phase 4*

THE PERFORMANCE

This final phase is to enable teachers to put a complicated piece of work together as a performance. This particular piece lends itself well to the use of costume, beads and face paint. Try to photograph or video the performance to aid subsequent work and also the study of Africa.

GROUP ORGANISATION

The whole class can perform this piece at the same time. However, it may be interesting to assign different roles to different individuals/groups of pupils, e.g. some members of the group only perform the **individual phrase** while others only perform the **mirror phrase** or group phrase. During the phases of inactivity pupils may like to find a suitable African war pose to freeze in, until it is their turn to perform again. All pupils should perform the introduction and finale as these are both important focal points and give balance to the performance.

It is also possible to divide the class into groups to enable the entire dance to be performed to the others. This gives all pupils the opportunity to experience both performance and audience skills.

Musical structure

00 – 10sec.   **Introduction**
Choose a starting position, wobble and vibrate this position to finish standing, facing the front.

11 – 55sec.   **Individual phrase**
Repeat the individual motif 6 times, twice at the front, then turning clockwise until returning to the front. Use the remainder of this phase to show other ways of moving to the rhythm, e.g. lunge/jump.

56sec. –   **Mirror phrase** in pairs
1min. 48sec.   Repeat the mirroring sequence, paying particular attention to the development of the rhythm.

1min. 49sec. – **Group phrase** in fours
2min. 04sec.   The **psst, psst** sound within a count of 8 identifies this phase of opposite movements and changes in level (x 4).

2min. 05sec. – **War cry – Wow uhh wow uhh** – free expression.
2min. 14sec.

2min. 15sec. – A continuation of **Group phrase** in fours (x 4)
2min. 31sec.

2min. 32sec. – Repeat **Mirror phrase** in pairs. Possibly focus on
3min. 33sec.   different pairs.

3min. 34sec. – **Individual phrase** repeated, as the music retraces
3min. 58sec.   its steps towards the finale.

3min. 59sec. – **Finale**
4min. 15sec.   Dramatic individual free expression.

GLOSSARY

Abstract dance	Free expression, improvisation or movement without structure.
Aesthetic appearance	Visual appearance of the performance.
Aesthetic appreciation	How the audience perceives the visual appearance of a performance.
Audience skills	Observation, listening and appreciation of ideas and presentation.
Balance	Stillness/shape held for a minimum of three seconds.
Body awareness	A confidence gained from co-ordination, balance, poise and timing.
Body parts	Leading body parts, trailing body parts, focal point of movement.
Body tension	Required to hold the body still to form a balance and essential to presentation, e.g. posture.
Canon	In a group, a motif which is repeated one person after the other, e.g. Mexican wave.
Core motif	The chorus or central movement pattern, motif or phrase, which may be repeated or modified throughout the dance.
Dance drama	A dance which tells a story, using characters, props and/or costumes.
Formation	Group pattern, e.g. line or lines, circle facing in or out, triangle.
Gesture	Use of the body, e.g. hands, to communicate instructions, feelings and moods.
Group dynamics	How the people within a group interact, e.g. some are static, while others move in space; some take a lead role, while others follow.
Group structure	The number of people within a group.
Level changes	Grow and rise, shrink and sink, open and close, forwards and back.
Mark	To go through the movements slowly, often using small motions to spark the memory, while counting in the head.
Motif	A gesture or action which is repeated often throughout a sequence.

Movement vocabulary	Developing ways of moving and stillness which enable more complex sequences to be created.
Performance skills	Presentation, quality, timing and enjoyment.
Phase	A section of work which links well together. This can be taught in one or more lesson blocks.
Phrase	Two or more motifs linked together to form a phrase.
Posture	Body tension, confidence and body awareness.
Power	Intensity of movement, e.g. strong or light.
Quality	Characteristic of movement, e.g. firm, energetic, light, flowing.
Rhythm	Flow of movement, e.g. fast or slow, simple or complicated.
Shape	Form of movement, e.g. tall, wide, narrow, small, stretched, twisted, curled, symmetric, asymmetric.
Simultaneous	Different movements or motifs occurring at the same time.
Size	Group or movement size, from small through to large.
Spatial awareness	Movement in space without collision, which also affects group dynamics, i.e. an awareness of one's body in relation to others.
Speed	Movements can be fast, slow, or a combination.
Static	Being still; a frozen shape or balance.
Structured dance	Set or predetermined patterns of steps/motifs, e.g. core motif.
Style	Type of movement, e.g. abstract, structured or dance drama.
Tension and relaxation	How the body moves/holds stillness and balance.
Timing	Movements or stillness in relation to the music and the other performers.
Travel	Gesture, motif and phrases which occur on the move, not static.
Unison	Movement or stillness which occurs at the same time.

APPENDIX

CUE CARDS FOR 'FIRE'

Flicker	Hissing
Fiercely	Leaping
Spitting	Writhing
Dancing	Darting
Twisting	Crackle
Devouring	Energy

CUE CARDS FOR 'THE SEA'

Sharp	Thin
Rough	Long
Soaring	Smooth
Gliding	Flight
Slippery	Watching
Wriggling	Swooping

Soft **Outstretched Wings**

Jagged **Holes**

Slimy **Diving**

CUE CARDS FOR 'THE LITTLE PRINCE'

BAOBABS

Entwined **Strong**

Thick **Twisted**

Angular **Tall**

ROSE

Magma   **Lava**   **Vent**

Bubbling   **Eruption**

Crater   **Active**   **Hot**

Dormant   **Pressure**

Melted   **Ash**   **Force**

CUE CARDS FOR 'BLUE'

OBJECTS – THE SEA

Ebb & flow   **Waves**

Spray   **Current**

OBJECTS – THE SKY

Birds   **Kites**

Leaves   **Clouds**

OBJECTS – BLUEBELL

Seed   **Shoot**

Stem   **Open petals**

OBJECTS   CHELSEA FC

Kick   Pass   Stop

Crowd chanting

Score/save a goal

Team celebration

SAYINGS – BLUE WITH THE COLD

Shiver   Huddle

Hit arms on sides

Wrap arms around

Wiggle fingers

Jog on the spot

Sharp intake of breath

SAYINGS – BLUE IN THE FACE

Anger   Shouting

Stamping   Punching

Fist waving

Tense shoulders

Facial expression

SAYINGS – OUT OF THE BLUE

Unexpected   **Surprise**

Shock   **Step back!**

Arms thrown up

Fingers wide apart

SAYINGS – BLUE BLOOD

Royal   **Regal**

Ceremonial   **Poise**

Procession

Bow/curtsey

Royal wave

FEELINGS AND EMOTIONS – FEELING EMOTION

Low **Sad**

Depressed

Empty **Down**

Low Energy

FEELINGS AND EMOTIONS – SHOWING EMOTION

Head in hands

Hang head

Crouch low

Curled up on floor

Chin on inside of hands

Slow movements/steps

Drooped shoulders

Scuff feet

Cheek on fist

Curl up and rock

CUE CARDS FOR 'AFRICAN DANCE' / FIRE

Arms	**Hands**
Fists	**Feet**
Ankles	**Knees**
Hips	**Legs**
Shoulders	**Head**
Elbows	